Peak Productivity
Strategies for Maintaining Focus

Joyce Pearl Campbell

Table of Contents

1. Introduction 2
2. Understanding Focus in the Digital Age 3
   2.1. The Evolution of Focus 3
   2.2. The Impact of Digital Distractions 3
   2.3. Coping Strategies in the Digital Age 4
   2.4. The Role of Mindful Living 5
3. The Art of Multitasking: Debunking the Myth 6
   3.1. The illusion of Multitasking 6
   3.2. Costs of Multitasking 7
   3.3. Single-Tasking as a Smart Strategy 7
   3.4. Methods for Effective Single-Tasking 8
4. Importance of Setting Purposeful Goals 9
   4.1. Understanding Purposeful Goals 9
   4.2. The Mechanics of Creating Purposeful Goals 10
   4.3. Transforming Goals into Reality 11
   4.4. Celebrating the Journey 11
5. Mindfulness: Cultivating Your Inner Focus 13
   5.1. Meditation: The Path to Mindfulness 13
   5.2. The Neuropsychology of Mindfulness 14
   5.3. Putting Mindfulness into Practice 14
   5.4. The Power of Mindful Eating 15
   5.5. Incorporating Mindfulness in Everyday Tasks 15
6. Strategies to Beat Procrastination 17
   6.1. Understanding and Accepting Your Procrastination 17
   6.2. Breaking Down Your Tasks 18
   6.3. Prioritizing Your Tasks 18
   6.4. Eliminating Distractions 19
   6.5. Using Positive Reinforcement 19

- 6.6. Cultivating Mindfulness … 19
- 7. Maintaining Work-Life Balance for Sustainable Productivity … 21
  - 7.1. The Rationale Behind Work-Life Balance … 21
  - 7.2. Analyzing and Prioritizing Tasks … 22
  - 7.3. Embracing Flexibility and Adaptability … 22
  - 7.4. The Role of Personal Well-being … 22
  - 7.5. The Power of Efficient Time Management … 23
- 8. Harnessing the Power of Flow State … 24
  - 8.1. Understanding the Flow State … 24
  - 8.2. The Benefits of Harnessing the Flow State … 25
  - 8.3. Strategies to Enter and Foster Flow State … 25
- 9. Embracing Breaks: Productivity Through Rest … 27
  - 9.1. The Science Behind Productivity and Rest … 27
  - 9.2. The Importance of Mind Wandering … 27
  - 9.3. The Role of Micro-Breaks … 28
  - 9.4. The Power of Napping … 28
  - 9.5. Digital Detox Breaks … 28
  - 9.6. Active Rest … 29
- 10. The Role of Physical Fitness in Enhancing Focus … 30
  - 10.1. The Science Behind Physical Fitness and Focus … 30
  - 10.2. Selective Physical Activities for Enhanced Focus … 31
  - 10.3. Implementing a Physical Fitness Routine … 32
  - 10.4. Conclusion … 32
- 11. Enhancing Productivity: Leveraging Apps and Digital Tools … 34
  - 11.1. The Rise of Digital Tools: A Narrative of Necessity … 34
  - 11.2. Understanding Your Needs: Picking the Right Tools … 34
  - 11.3. Collaboration Platforms … 35
  - 11.4. Time Management Tools … 35
  - 11.5. Task Management Software … 35
  - 11.6. Health-Focused Apps … 36

11.7. Making it Work: Integrating Digital Tools in Your Routine .. 36
11.8. The Flip Side: Avoiding App Overload 36

Concentrate all your thoughts upon the work at hand. The sun's rays do not burn until brought to a focus.

— Alexander Graham Bell

Chapter 1. Introduction

In our rapidly moving world, maintaining focus can feel like an uphill battle amidst a gamut of distractions and life pressures. Don't be discouraged, you are not alone, and we have the perfect tool to help you conquer this challenge. Welcome to our Special Report on "Peak Productivity: Strategies for Maintaining Focus"! This enthusiastic guide will equip you with productive practices, innovative strategies, and insightful tips geared towards holding your attention and maximizing your output. Whether you're an entrepreneur, a creative artist, a busy parent, or a diligent student, this Special Report holds the key to unlocking your full potential and propelling you towards your life goals. Get ready to transform your work-life experience into a triumph of productivity by delving into this exciting offering. Your journey towards peak productivity is just a purchase away! So why wait? Let's get started on achieving more by building unyielding focus.

Chapter 2. Understanding Focus in the Digital Age

"Peak Productivity: Strategies for Maintaining Focus" begins with a deep dive into the first colossal topic enhancing our quest for superior productivity: Understanding Focus in the Digital Age. The rapid development of digital technology and the increasing integration of the Internet and social media into our daily lives have fundamentally altered our traditional ways of focusing on tasks and information processing. This chapter's objective is to break down, analyze, and scrutinize these changes and devise strategies to navigate the novel demands of our digital era.

2.1. The Evolution of Focus

Our capacity to stay attentive and concentrate on a specific task or thought is what we refer to as focus. Since prehistoric times, human beings have been gradually evolving their cognitive abilities according to their changing environments and necessities. Initiating with the hunter-gatherers' need to focus intently on physical tasks for survival and evolving into an era where focus is required for more abstract and complex intellectual tasks.

In the modern Information Age, the proliferation of digital technology and a deluge of information has transformed our lifestyle. Consequently, the nature of focus has also morphically evolved, posing both opportunities and challenges.

2.2. The Impact of Digital Distractions

With the digital transformation, we have seen increased levels of interruption. Each digital ping, tweet, email, message, or alert, pulls your attention away from whatever you're currently engaged in. These disruptions, although seemingly mundane and tolerable, gradually add up and significantly affect your productivity.

Research suggests that once interrupted, it can take up to 20 minutes for the human brain to regain its focus and concentration. Therefore, the impact of these digital distractions is not trivial, and understanding this phenomenon is essential for devising strategies to guard against the continuous interruptions that come with the digital age.

2.3. Coping Strategies in the Digital Age

Now that we have identified the problem, the next step is to look for solutions. There are numerous strategies to cope with the challenges imposed by the digital age.

Firstly, consider 'Digital Detox,' a period in which you disconnect from digital devices, allowing your mind to rest and rejuvenate from constant stimuli bombardment.

Secondly, 'Single-Tasking' is a principle that champions focusing on one task at a time. Research has proven that constant multi-tasking reduces focus and productivity, further reinforcing the importance of single-tasking.

Finally, use productivity apps or tools like 'Pomodoro Technique,' a time-management method encouraging people to work with time rather than against it. Dividing your work into 25 minutes intervals with 5-minute breaks allows the brain to focus effectively and enhance productivity.

2.4. The Role of Mindful Living

Mindfulness is the practice of maintaining a moment-by-moment awareness of our thoughts, feelings, bodily sensations, and the surrounding environment.

In the modern digital age, practicing mindfulness can be instrumental in strengthening our focus. In the face of constant digital noise, it helps us differentiate between important information and distractions. It allows us to slow down our mental processes and focus on the present task at hand. By managing our attention skillfully, we can filter out irrelevant distractions and focus on what is truly important.

In conclusion, understanding focus in the digital age is not a straightforward task due to the subtle and complex changes brought about by digital technologies and an information-saturated world. However, by dissecting this issue and developing effective coping strategies, it is entirely possible to reclaim our ability to focus and, in turn, enhance our productivity.

Chapter 3. The Art of Multitasking: Debunking the Myth

Delving into the fascinating realm of productivity strategies and cognitive exploration, we first encounter the alluring yet widely misunderstood concept of multitasking. But is it truly the productivity panacea we've been led to believe? Unfortunately, the evidence suggests otherwise. This chapter aims to uncover the truth, debunk the myth, and explore why our brains are not designed for multitasking in the way that modern society often demands.

3.1. The illusion of Multitasking

More often than not, multitasking is hailed as a covetable skill in our buzzing world of professional and personal pursuits. In the modern age where the influx of data is overwhelming, the ability to handle multiple tasks simultaneously seems indispensable. The word itself emanates an aura of efficiency; an ability to gracefully juggle several duties, embodying the quintessential productivity guru. However, truth be told, multitasking is more of an illusion than a reality.

Research into this area by cognitive scientists reveals that what we perceive as multitasking is, in reality, task-switching. Our brains switch from one task to another rapidly, giving the illusion of doing multiple tasks simultaneously. The brain is not designed to handle two high cognitive load tasks simultaneously. It's incapable of processing two streams of information concurrently, of the same type, at full capacity.

3.2. Costs of Multitasking

The drawbacks of multitasking are manifold. For starters, it leads to an increase in errors. As attention is dispersed between several tasks, the quality of work created by a 'multitasking' mind can often be compromised. Delving deeper into the cognitive neuroscience behind it, when our brains switch tasks, they utilize more energy and create room for errors.

In addition, the act of multitasking often leads to mental fatigue, with constant task-switching being taxing on the mind. More alarmingly, a chronic reliance on multitasking can have a long-term impact on brain density, particularly in areas related to empathy and emotional control, according to studies.

NASA's research drills the point further home. Pilots who multitask are more likely to miss critical signals compared to those who focus intently on one task. Essentially, the costs of multitasking are high, and it is far from being a productivity booster.

3.3. Single-Tasking as a Smart Strategy

If multitasking is not the key to peak productivity, what is? The answer lies in single-tasking, a term which may lack the glamour of its multitasking counterpart but is backed by a growing body of scientific research. Single-tasking involves focusing on one task at a time, giving it the undiluted attention it deserves. It goes hand in hand with mindfulness, allowing you to immerse yourself in the task at hand fully, leading to a marked increase in productivity and work quality.

Simply put, single-tasking is about enjoying the present moment and deriving satisfaction from the task at hand. It's about being 'in the moment', everytime. When your focus is unwavering, your energy is harnessed into the task, leading to a better output.

3.4. Methods for Effective Single-Tasking

One of the most effective ways to cultivate single-tasking and elevate your productivity is to apply three strategies: Prioritize your tasks, time-block, and take breaks.

1. *Prioritize your tasks*: Not all tasks hold the same importance. By learning to articulate your priorities and focusing on one task at a time, you can ensure that your energy is directed towards the tasks that matter most.
2. *Time-block*: Assign a specific time block for each task. This method encourages focus by designating a certain period for a single task, removing the temptation of task-switching.
3. *Take breaks*: Breaks are integral for maintaining concentration and staving off mental fatigue. A well-known productivity technique, the Pomodoro Technique, encourages taking a brief five-minute break every 25 minutes to refresh and recharge your mind.

In conclusion, multitasking is more of a myth than a miracle. It is a master of illusion, tricking us into believing we are doing more when we are, in reality, achieving less. The secret to peak productivity might not be hidden in fancy jargon or glamorous techniques but in the simple and mindful act of single-tasking. By debunking the myth of multitasking and reinstating the power of focusing on one task at a time, we open ourselves to a more organic and effective way of working, leading to unprecedented productivity and success.

Chapter 4. Importance of Setting Purposeful Goals

Goals give purpose and direction to our life. They provide a compass, guiding our actions and choices towards meaningful accomplishments. Without defined goals, we often find ourselves swallowed by the monotony and random whims of our everyday existence. It's almost akin to launching spear after spear into an abyss and hoping we strike a target. But by setting purposeful goals, we transform that abyss into a visible bullseye, giving our efforts a clear path, direction, and a tangible endpoint.

4.1. Understanding Purposeful Goals

Purposeful goals are more than a mere benchmark of achievement. They represent the deep-seated aspirations that kindle our internal flame, invoke our authentic passions and inherent values. These are the goals that truly matter to us and derive from our personal ambitions, not societal expectations. They are long-term, definitive, and organically intertwined with our identity, ultimately giving form to our life's mission statement.

A common scenario is setting a goal to make a certain sum of money. However, the true purpose behind such a goal is often to gain financial freedom, security, or the means to support loved ones. Hence, the financial goal is simply a vector toward the larger, purposeful goal.

The first step towards setting purposeful goals is introspection. Delving deep into the core of our aspirations, we must ask ourselves - what do we genuinely want to achieve in our lifetime? What ignites our passion and motivates us to strive continuously? By answering these questions, we start peeling back the layers, revealing our authentic ambitions.

4.2. The Mechanics of Creating Purposeful Goals

Once we have understood the essence of purposeful goals, the subsequent step is to articulate them. Articulating a goal brings clarity and precision, while also facilitating the operational planning of strategies to achieve it.

One effective technique for creating precise and achievable goals is the SMART framework. SMART stands for Specific, Measurable, Attainable, Relevant, and Time-bound. Let's delve deep into this approach:

- Specific: This pertains to the precision and clarity of the goal. An ambiguous goal like 'I want to be successful' can be made specific by revisiting the definition of success, such as 'I want to launch a best-selling novel within the next two years.'

- Measurable: This implies the ability to quantify or qualify progress. It provides feedback, helping adjust strategies if required. For example, instead of 'I want to eat healthier,' use 'I want to incorporate five servings of fruits and vegetables into my daily diet.'

- Attainable: A goal should be challenging yet achievable, considering resources, abilities, and circumstances. Setting an overly unrealistic goal can lead to frustration and, eventually, abandonment.

- Relevant: A goal should be meaningful and align with larger objectives and values. A goal that seems irrelevant can lack conviction and motivation, derailing consistent effort.

- Time-bound: Setting a time frame helps maintain focus and urgency, preventing procrastination and complacency. It provides a clear endpoint, contributing to a sense of accomplishment upon completion.

4.3. Transforming Goals into Reality

The journey between goal-setting and goal-achievement is filled with potential hurdles and unpredictability. So, it's crucial to create a robust action plan that incorporates contingencies, reinforcing our commitment to the finish line. Contingency planning helps anticipate possible obstacles, preparing us to face unexpected challenges and sway them into opportunities.

Moreover, breaking down the overall goal into manageable sub-goals or milestones can avoid overwhelm and maintain momentum. Each milestone achieved provides positive reinforcement and a sense of progress, keeping us motivated.

It's also vital to maintain flexibility while pursuing these goals. Rigidity can hinder progress, escalate stress, and perhaps even lead to burnout. Adopting a Growth Mindset, which embraces failures as opportunities for learnings and adjustments, can be transformational in the journey towards goal attainment.

Remember, achievement comes with an inherent learning curve and moving towards your goals will invariably involve days of stagnation, frustration, and even failure. However, it's critical to perceive these as stepping stones towards success rather than insurmountable roadblocks.

4.4. Celebrating the Journey

The significance of celebrating milestones in our journey cannot be understated. These celebrations are not merely about the achievement but about acknowledging the perseverance, the effort, and the will power that it took to surpass each step. They offer a moment of rest, satisfaction, and motivation to push through the next set of challenges.

In conclusion, purposeful goal setting is not just about reaching an endpoint, but it's about embracing the journey, the personal growth, and the transformative experiences that come along. It's a cornerstone of living a fulfilling life, filled with purpose, passion, and prodigious productivity. So, prod yourself on, set your purposeful goals, and embark on a journey of self-discovery, achievement, and unparalleled satisfaction.

Chapter 5. Mindfulness: Cultivating Your Inner Focus

At the very heart of the bustling demands of our modern world, amid the myriad of tasks and overlapping responsibilities, there lies an oasis of serene tranquility, a quietude that is vital for maintaining robust focus. This sanctuary is not a geographical place, but rather a certain state of mind, a mindful presence. To break it down to its essence, mindfulness is the practice of deliberately paying attention to what's happening in the present moment without judgment. It is this essence that forms the indispensable body of today's discourse on inner focus cultivation.

5.1. Meditation: The Path to Mindfulness

Before diving deep into the complexities of mindfulness, it is crucial to understand the key vehicle leading to this state: meditation. The practice of meditation - as old as civilization itself - is arguably the most effective means of developing mindfulness. While it bears various forms, all involve the fundamental element of directing self-awareness towards one's inner world.

A specific form of meditation that has gained popularity in recent times is 'Mindfulness-Based Stress Reduction' or MBSR. This method follows the teaching of Jon Kabat-Zinn, who rationalizes meditation as an exercise in sustaining attention on a chosen object of focus - often the breath, thoughts, or bodily sensations. The moment distraction begins to creep in, the practice instructs returning the attention gently back to the designated focus. Thus imbuing individuals with discernable cognitive resilience and an enhanced capacity for focus.

5.2. The Neuropsychology of Mindfulness

From the neuroscience perspective, mindfulness alters the brain's structure and function systematically, contributing significantly to sustained focus and attention. Scientists have found that consistent mindfulness practice results in enhanced attentional control, working memory capacity, and cognitive flexibility - all crucial factors nurturing our ability to focus.

Research conducted on experienced meditators demonstrates an increased cortical thickness in the prefrontal cortex and right anterior insula. These cerebral regions are primarily associated with attention, introspection, and sensory processing. Furthermore, studies reveal that mindfulness training can significantly reduce activity in our default mode network (DMN), a neural network responsible for mind-wandering, usually linked with unhappiness and worry.

5.3. Putting Mindfulness into Practice

The concept of mindfulness is easy to comprehend but often challenging to implement. For starters, it is recommended to choose a quiet and comfortable space for daily meditation practice. Sessions can vary from five to thirty minutes, gradually increased as comfort grows with experience. Regularity, rather than lengthy sessions, enhances the impact of mindfulness practice.

The act of meditation commences by closing the eyes and removing all external distractions. The individual then commences taking slow, deep breaths, focusing attention on the sensation of air entering and exiting the body. As inevitable distractions (thoughts, feelings, sensations) arise, the practitioner develops resilience in restoring focus back to the breath.

An essential aspect of mindfulness lies in realizing that thoughts and emotions are transient. They come and go, and are not an integral part of us, allowing to 'defuse' from them and view them objectively. This 'meta-cognitive' realization imparts a rich clarity, embellishing the individual's ability to discern, focus, and engage profoundly with tasks at hand.

5.4. The Power of Mindful Eating

One often overlooked area when cultivating mindfulness revolves around our relationship with food. Mindful eating means fully dedicating your focus to the act of eating, savoring each bite, recognizing the food's tastes and smells, and acknowledging the nourishment it brings. By enhancing sensory awareness during mealtime, not only do you enhance enjoyment and satisfaction, but you also improve focus and attention as extraneous distractions are minimised.

5.5. Incorporating Mindfulness in Everyday Tasks

Finally, an integral part of cultivating mindfulness is embracing the practice in daily activities beyond the boundaries of formal meditation. Simple activities like washing dishes, taking a walk, brushing your teeth, or even waiting for an appointment can be transformed into opportunities for mindfulness practice. By fostering a non-judgmental awareness and presence in seemingly mundane activities, we cultivate an enriched reservoir of focus and attention, ready to be employed in any task that requires it.

In essence, the journey of cultivating mindfulness as a tool for enhancing focus is a profound exploration of self-awareness and resilience. It is a journey of uncovering the power of the present moment, of transcending the noisy distractions of our surrounding environment, and deliberately directing our focus towards the task at hand. It is an endeavor that promises the invaluable rewards of clarity, resilience, and, eventually, peak productivity.

Chapter 6. Strategies to Beat Procrastination

Procrastination, the bane of productivity, is a formidable adversary standing in the way of many people's goals. Confronting and overcoming this foe opens an array of opportunities to enhance overall productivity. This journey towards defeating procrastination calls for an intricate tangle of strategies, which, when implemented methodically, can lead to impeccable results. These are strategies that aren't far-reaching in their complexity, but rather grounded in their practical and immediate application. Let us step into this comprehensive deep dive into the arsenal of strategies needed in our campaign to beat procrastination.

6.1. Understanding and Accepting Your Procrastination

Procrastination derives from a variety of sources. Identifying these driving forces is an essential step in forming our battle plan. Fear of failure can often deter us from beginning tasks, leading to a cycle of procrastination. Likewise, overwhelmed individuals who face many complex tasks may opt to delay action. Personal disorganization and distraction susceptibility also significantly contribute to procrastination.

The first step to overcome procrastination is to acknowledge its presence. Ignorance here is not bliss. It is vital to confront the fact that task delay happens. Once acceptance occurs, understanding why it happens becomes the next hurdle. To identify the reasons behind procrastination, maintaining a procrastination log can prove beneficial. This record should note each instance of procrastination; what task was postponed, when and why it occurred. Over time, you will start to uncover the patterns leading to your avoidance.

6.2. Breaking Down Your Tasks

Large, complex tasks can steer us towards procrastination due to their daunting nature. The solution to counteract this feeling lies in breaking down tasks into manageable subtasks. This subdivision not only makes the overall project feel less intimidating but also allows for easier tracking of progress.

Each subtask's accomplishment can be viewed as a small victory, boosting your confidence and offering a sense of achievement that further motivates you to remain focused and persistently forge ahead.

6.3. Prioritizing Your Tasks

Having a roadmap guides us through our day's tasks and significantly discourages procrastination. An effective method to construct this roadmap is the Eisenhower Box, inspired by former U.S. President Dwight D. Eisenhower.

The Eisenhower box is divided into four sections:

- Urgent and important
- Important but not urgent
- Urgent but not important
- Not urgent and not important

By categorizing your tasks into these sections, you can discern the order of priority in which they need to be completed. This segregation lifts the burden of uncertainty and prepares your mind to approach tasks in an organized manner.

6.4. Eliminating Distractions

Your environment heavily influences your ability to concentrate on your tasks. A cluttered workspace can lead to a cluttered mind and, by extension, encourage procrastination. Maintaining a tidy, clean workplace or study area sets a positive ambiance for effective concentration.

Furthermore, the integration of technology into daily life offers myriad opportunities for distraction. Countless applications and websites can divert attention from the task at hand, feeding procrastination. A proactive measure against this effect is the use of apps that block certain websites during designated working hours or keep track of time spent on different devices.

6.5. Using Positive Reinforcement

Rewarding yourself after completing a task acts as an incentive. This strategy employs a form of operant conditioning that fosters eagerness towards task completion and reduces instances of procrastination. The rewards can range from a short break, a treat, or even an episode of beloved TV show.

However, it is critical to ensure that the rewards are appropriate and proportional to the task's size and difficulty. Over-rewarding simple tasks may prove counterproductive as it might lead to overly long breaks or rewards becoming the sole focus rather than task completion.

6.6. Cultivating Mindfulness

Mindfulness aids in remaining steadfast in the present moment allowing full engagement in the task at hand. This mental state decreases the likelihood of distraction and, therefore, procrastination. Methods to achieve mindfulness include meditation, yoga, or even just taking slow, deep breaths when you feel distracted or overwhelmed.

By utilizing these strategies, we can systematically break the shackles of procrastination and stride towards our aspirations with newfound momentum. By doing so, it's important to remember that overcoming procrastination is not an overnight success story. It requires patience, persistence, and a touch of self-compassion when we experience setbacks. But it's worth the effort, as, in the journey of defeating procrastination, we are indeed unearthing a treasure box of productivity, alignment, and achievement.

Chapter 7. Maintaining Work-Life Balance for Sustainable Productivity

Few aspects of modern life can grow to be as demanding as surfacing a solid balance between work and life commitments. To begin understanding the nuances of maintaining this equilibrium, it's important to comprehend the concept of work-life balance. Fundamentally, it's about allowing time for and significance to all aspects of life, such as work, personal interests, family and social engagements. Achieving this balance is, without a doubt, the backbone of sustainable productivity. Enabling a well-rounded life not only results in improved personal health and happiness, but it also catalyzes the potential for a significant productivity increase in your professional environment.

7.1. The Rationale Behind Work-Life Balance

- Work-life balance is not a one-size-fits-all concept. It varies wildly from person to person based on their personalities, work habits, personal commitments, and overall life goals; however, unanimously, efficiency experts concur that maintaining a healthy work-life balance is fundamental to long-term productivity and personal well-being. Striking the perfect equilibrium can ensure perpetual energy, unswerving focus, job satisfaction, and overall enjoyment in life. However, inability or negligence towards this can lead to burnout, stress, unhappiness, and ultimately decreased productivity—a counterproductive scenario for everyone involved.

7.2. Analyzing and Prioritizing Tasks

In the quest to achieve work-life balance for sustainable productivity, task prioritization is a critical first step. By understanding the importance and urgency of each task, one can allocate time accordingly, ensuring the most critical tasks receive the attention they deserve first.

To segregate tasks effectively, employ a tool such as the Eisenhower Matrix, which splits tasks into four categories: Do first (important and urgent), Schedule (important but not urgent), Delegate (not important but urgent), and Don't do (not important, not urgent). Applying such a strategic approach can substantially alleviate the stress of juggling multiple tasks and, in turn, contribute to an improved work-life balance.

7.3. Embracing Flexibility and Adaptability

Promoting flexibility and encouraging adaptability in your professional life can beneficially impact your work-life balance. This involves letting go of rigidity in how tasks are completed and instead focusing more on accomplishing outcomes.

For example, embrace remote or telecommuting work options when available, adjust your working hours to fit your lifestyle better, or upskill yourself to handle a variety of tasks. This flexibility often allows for more personal time and reduces stress, leading to a more balanced life and improved productivity.

7.4. The Role of Personal Well-being

Personal well-being is a crucial component in the pursuit of work-life balance. Without taking proper care of your physical and mental health, achieving a balanced life becomes increasingly challenging. Regular exercise, a balanced diet, quality sleep, and mindfulness practices contribute significantly towards overall wellness.

Furthermore, activities, such as hobbies, social engagements, or simply spending time with loved ones, can go a long way in ensuring mental vitality. Since a healthier mind and body increase energy levels, motivation, and focus, they indirectly contribute to heightened productivity.

7.5. The Power of Efficient Time Management

Efficient time management is undoubtedly one of the most potent strategies for maintaining a healthy work-life balance. By consciously controlling the amount of time dedicated to specific activities, one can enhance productivity and create space for leisure time, self-improvement, or relaxation.

Adopting tools like time tracking apps, calendars, and productivity software can greatly contribute towards dividing your time efficiently for different tasks and activities. Similarly, techniques like the Pomodoro Technique, time blocking, or the 80/20 rule can significantly enhance productivity and leave more room for life outside work.

In conclusion, maintaining a healthy work-life balance is not only desirable but a must for sustainable productivity. It necessitates consistent effort and intent to prioritize tasks, promote flexibility, care for personal well-being, and manage time efficiently. Once achieved, work-life balance paves the way for enhanced productivity that is sustainable, satisfying, and incredibly fulfilling.

Chapter 8. Harnessing the Power of Flow State

Flow state, often referred to as "being in the zone," is an elusive yet immensely powerful state of being where individual productivity and creativity reach their highest peaks. This psychological condition occurs when one is fully engaged in a task, where the world and its myriad distractions fade away, replaced by a singular focus and absorption in the task at hand.

Harnessing this state of sublime immersion is not an effortless endeavor. It requires an alignment of various physical, mental, and environmental factors. Therefore, in this chapter, we shall delve into the mechanics of the flow state, its benefits, and strategies focusing on how to enter this powerful state, as well as how to make it a more frequent visitor in your productivity toolkit.

8.1. Understanding the Flow State

As a concept, the flow state has its foundational blocks in positive psychology, the brain child of Hungarian-American psychologist, Mihaly Csikszentmihalyi. He describes flow as an ecstatic state where an individual wholly immerses in an activity that they relish so much, that they lose track of time and the external world around them, focusing solely on the task at hand.

As an analogy, imagine a musician lost in their performance, or an artist engrossed in their creation, or even an athlete in the heat of competition. All these individuals have transcended the realm of distractions, insecurities, and self-doubt to reach a state where they are at peak performance, utterly absorbed in their respective tasks.

Flow state has several characteristic elements which include: * Intense concentration on the task at hand * A sense of effortlessness and ease in the activity * Losing track of time * Receiving immediate feedback * A balance between the challenge of the task and personal skill levels * A sense of control over the task

When these elements coincide, they create the flow state, which can become an essential component of personal productivity and fulfillment.

8.2. The Benefits of Harnessing the Flow State

One of the primary reasons why flow is beneficial for productivity lies in its positive impact on individual performance. Beyond just improving the quality and quantity of work, immersing oneself in a flow state can yield various other benefits:

- Increased Creativity: The flow state creates a fertile ground for innovative ideas and solutions to sprout and grow.
- Enhanced Performance: In a flow state, one's performance goes several notches higher, resulting in exceptional work quality.
- Greater Satisfaction: The flow states are not just about productivity; they also lead to improved satisfaction and happiness in one's work.
- Reduced stress and improved mental health: Achieving flow aids in mitigating anxiety and stress, contributing towards overall mental well-being.

8.3. Strategies to Enter and Foster Flow State

Harnessing the power of flow state requires an understanding of its enabling factors and a series of strategies that cultivate these. Here are a few techniques that can help you enter and maintain this powerful mental state:

1. **Identify Your Passion**: This may seem obvious, but engaging in tasks that engross, excite, or challenge you are more likely to trigger flow. It's essential to align your work and activities with your interests and abilities for this reason.

2. **Set Clear Goals**: In order to create the necessary structure and focus, it's crucial to create clear, achievable goals. Ideally, these will be tasks that present enough of a challenge to maintain engagement, without being overly extreme.

3. **Create a Distraction-Free Environment**: Flow thrives in an environment uncluttered by the disruptive noise of modern life. Find a quiet, comfortable place to work where interruptions are minimized.

4. **Seek Instant Feedback**: Feedback can be a powerful catalyst for flow, allowing individuals to adjust their performance and remain in the zone. Technology can often help provide real-time feedback on many tasks.

5. **Practice Mindfulness**: Cultivate mindfulness and increase your ability to become aware of the present moment. This skill will allow you to become fully absorbed in the task at hand, fostering the onset of flow.

The power of a flow state is extraordinary and can dramatically increase both your productivity and satisfaction with any given task. Understanding and cultivating flow can act as a pathway to both professional success and personal fulfillment.

Chapter 9. Embracing Breaks: Productivity Through Rest

At first glance, the connection between 'breaks' and 'productivity' might seem antithetical. You might ask, "Isn't productivity about relentless forward progress, a continual climb towards attainment of objectives?" However, as we delve deeper into this topic, you will encounter paradoxical wisdom that can fundamentally alter your perception of productivity. Taking regular breaks is not only beneficial, but also critical to maintaining peak productivity.

9.1. The Science Behind Productivity and Rest

To understand the co-relation between breaks and productivity, we must first acquaint ourselves with the scientific rationale. Research has shown that our brain operates in two modes: the 'focused mode', which we use when working or studying, and the 'diffuse mode', which is like a neurological autopilot where our minds wander. When we engage in deep work or learning, the neuron patterns in our brains get solidified, which can lead to cognitive fatigue. Breaks shift our brain to the diffuse mode, allowing the neurons to relax, reorient, and be ready for the next bout of intense focus. Over time, this rest-focused cycle contributes to the acquisition of new knowledge, the rejuvenation of cognitive abilities, and the enhancement of decision-making skills.

9.2. The Importance of Mind Wandering

Mind wandering, an aspect of the diffuse mode, has been vilified as a sign of inefficiency and lack of focus. But studies in cognitive neuroscience reveal a different story. It is during these periods of apparent aimlessness that the brain carries out essential maintenance activities. It consolidates memories, replenishes attention capacities, and kindles creativity. So, the next time your mind drifts off during a break, remember that it's an integral part of maintaining long-term productivity.

9.3. The Role of Micro-Breaks

Micro-breaks are short periods of relaxation in between tasks. Research conducted in fields such as organizational psychology underscores the benefit of these brief respites. Whether it's a quick stretch, a short walk, a moment of meditation, or simply gazing out of the window, micro-breaks help ward off the fatigue stemming from long periods of concentrated work. They alleviate mental strain, alleviate mood, and recharge cognitive capabilities, thus bolstering your productivity levels.

9.4. The Power of Napping

Napping is not just functional laziness; it has profound recuperative and restorative powers. A brief mid-day nap can do wonders for your productivity. It aids memory consolidation, increases alertness, enhances reaction time and boosts creativity. The key is strategic napping – aiming for a 'power nap' of around 15-20 minutes, which taps into the benefits of the lighter stages of sleep without leading to sleep inertia or grogginess.

9.5. Digital Detox Breaks

In our incessantly connected digital world, the power of disconnecting cannot be overstated. Scheduling digital detox breaks into your routine can help combat the side-effects of relentless screen time, including mental fatigue and impaired focus. It offers an opportunity to reconnect with the physical world and foster a healthy relationship with technology, thereby significantly ameliorating your overall productivity.

9.6. Active Rest

Integrating physical activity into your break periods is another effective means to refresh yourself. Activities such as walking, stretching, or light workouts can stimulate blood flow, enhance mental acuity, and boost energy levels. Even investing in an ergonomically friendly workspace with standing desks or treadmill desks can contribute to this active-rest concept.

This chapter has presented various facets of embracing breaks for productivity enhancement. Real productivity isn't about relentless toil; it's about sustainable efforts, punctuated by meaningful and intentional rest periods. It's about understanding your cognitive rhythms and using breaks strategically to bring forth your best work. Remember, in the realm of productivity, less can indeed be more. Rest up to ramp up, and your productivity would scale new pinnacles.

Chapter 10. The Role of Physical Fitness in Enhancing Focus

Physical fitness, an often overlooked element, plays an indispensable role in enhancing focus. The connection between the body and the mind is boundless; one profoundly influences the other. Whether you're an individual struggling to maintain focus amidst a hectic schedule, or someone hoping to maximize cognitive performance, physical activity presents itself as a tool to readjust attention, enhance intellect, and stimulate creativity.

10.1. The Science Behind Physical Fitness and Focus

The profound impact of physical fitness on our focus begins with the scientific correlation between the two. Biologically, physical exercises trigger an increase in heart rate, which ultimately leads to improved blood flow to the brain. This oxygen enrichment enables enhanced cognitive functioning, promotes better concentration, and augments learning capacity. Additionally, there's a release of endorphins, often referred to as 'feel-good' hormones, that help alleviate stress and anxiety, enhancing mental clarity and concentration.

Another key hormone produced during physical activity is the brain-derived neurotrophic factor (BDNF). Its primary role is to promote the survival of nerve cells (neurons) by playing a crucial part in growth, maturation (differentiation), and maintenance of these cells. Hence, improved BDNF levels don't just improve memory and thinking skills; they also contribute to better focus and increased concentration.

Furthermore, in various scientific studies, regular exercise has been associated with structural changes in the brain. These include an increase in gray matter volume particularly in regions involved with cognitive functions like attention control, working memory, and cognitive flexibility.

10.2. Selective Physical Activities for Enhanced Focus

Not all physical activities yield the same cognitive benefits. Some workouts are particularly known for their remarkable effects on mental focus and productivity. Below are a few exercises that are scientifically proven to boost your concentration and mental sharpness:

- **Aerobic Exercises:** Light to moderate aerobic exercises (such as jogging, cycling, or swimming) can increase creativity and problem-solving skills. They stimulate enhanced cerebral blood flow, thus positively influencing cognitive functions.
- **Yoga:** Practice of yoga combines physical postures, breath control, and meditation. It helps in reducing anxiety and stress, promoting relaxation, and significantly improving focus and attention.
- **Tai Chi:** This martial art form that originated from China involves making slow, graceful movements while breathing deeply. Studies show that Tai Chi can improve cognitive functions and enhance concentration in people of various age ranges.
- **Strength Training:** Engaging in strength training exercises can improve memory, attention, and the ability to resolve conflicts. Lifting weights isn't just for the bodybuilders, it's a surefire strategy to boost cognitive performance as well.

10.3. Implementing a Physical Fitness Routine

Aim to incorporate a blend of the aforementioned exercise types into your schedule. Building a balanced and habituated fitness routine is key to reaping enduring cognitive benefits. Start slow and gradually increase the intensity of your workout. It's crucial not to exhaust yourself physically, as this can be counterproductive, leading to fatigue, which in turn may decrease your focus.

Regular physical activity should be viewed not just as an investment in your physical health, but as critical preparation for intellectual tasks. Consider your exercise regime as mental training as much as it is physical.

The best routine is often the one we can stick to consistently. Create a fitness routine that works with your lifestyle, resources, and interests. Find an activity that you enjoy so that it does not feel like a chore, but instead becomes a pleasurable and rewarding experience. Over time, your frequency, intensity, and duration should increase as you build endurance and strength.

Remember, staying active also shows a direct relation to better sleep, another influential factor for improving concentration and reducing stress. Good quality and quantity of sleep will ensure your mind is well-rested and equipped for intense focus periods.

10.4. Conclusion

In conclusion, physical fitness is not just about building muscle or losing weight. The interdependence of our body and brain indicates that physical well-being can significantly enhance cognitive functioning, including focus. By understanding the science behind this relationship and implementing a targeted physical fitness routine, individuals are empowered to boost their mental acuity and productivity. Physical fitness is, therefore, an essential strategy in reaching peak productivity, regardless of the field you operate in. Embrace a physically active regime and watch as your life transforms, one focused moment at a time.

Chapter 11. Enhancing Productivity: Leveraging Apps and Digital Tools

In this technologically driven age, the way we operate and perform tasks has drastically shifted. There's arguably no realm this stands truer than when it comes to productivity enhancement. An array of digital tools, designed with the prime intention to streamline processes and operate more efficiently, have emerged in recent years and witnessed wide acceptance. From scheduling apps that organize your day to digital workspaces aimed at team collaboration, there's certainly no shortage of options. The trick, however, is knowing how to leverage these to your benefit.

11.1. The Rise of Digital Tools: A Narrative of Necessity

Born out of the need for efficient operations, digital tools are the children of modernity, rooted in the necessity to stay afloat amidst rapid advancements. As productivity became the holy grail of success, developers around the globe harnessed their technical wizardry to create apps and software that allow us to manage time wisely, delegate effectively, and promote a balanced life.

11.2. Understanding Your Needs: Picking the Right Tools

However, navigating through the ocean of digital tools can be overwhelming. Considering the criticality of choosing the right apps – ones that align with your work pattern, lifestyle, and nature of tasks, it's essential to understand precisely what you need. Maybe you are a team of one and require tools for task management, or perhaps you coordinate a global team evidencing the need for a collaboration tool equipped with features for seamless communication.

11.3. Collaboration Platforms

When it comes to managing a team or collaborative work, tools like Slack, Microsoft Teams, or Asana lead the way. These platforms provide a unified space for tasks assigning, progress tracking, file sharing, and real-time communication, resulting in increased transparency and efficiency. They not only pool resources together but also instill a sense of accountability among team members.

11.4. Time Management Tools

On the flip side, if it's about organizing your day, balancing between professional commitments, and carving out time for relaxation or hobbies, apps like Google Calendar, Toggl, or TimeTree might be your saviors. Their features include setting reminders, blocking periods for specific tasks, integrating with other tools, and generating reports to understand better how you're spending your time.

11.5. Task Management Software

For the more task-oriented individual or team, apps like Trello, Todoist, or Notion can be a boon. These tools have features like kanban boards, checklists, and priority settings, which help visualize and manage your workflow effectively. They can also integrate with collaboration platforms or calendar apps, providing a holistic productivity enhancement experience.

11.6. Health-Focused Apps

In the line-up of digital tools, never underestimate the value of health-focused apps that can monitor your sleep patterns, remind you to drink water, or guide you through quick workout routines. Apps like MyFitnessPal, Headspace, or Sleep Cycle can play a crucial role in maintaining well-being and consequently enhancing productivity.

11.7. Making it Work: Integrating Digital Tools in Your Routine

While these tools provide a robust lineup of features, the success of leveraging them lies in effective incorporation into your routine. It's recommended to gradually introduce them into your workflow rather than trying to juggle multiple new tools simultaneously. An initial time investment in understanding the functionalities and customizing the settings to your preference could go a long way in ensuring you reap maximum benefits.

11.8. The Flip Side: Avoiding App Overload

While it's enticing to try all the shiny new apps on the productivity shelf, a balanced approach is critical. Trying to integrate too many tools simultaneously can lead to 'app overload,' leaving you overwhelmed and counterproductively distracted. Remember, the aim is enhancing productivity, not mastering the art of using every tool available.

As we conclude, it's crucial to recognize that while these digital aids can help enhance productivity, they're merely facilitators, not the solution itself. The effectiveness of these tools depends largely on your commitment to your goals, your persistence in establishing productive habits, and, most importantly, your willingness to adapt and learn. While we have entered a digital age, the human elements of self-discipline, dedication, and drive underpin true productivity. So, leverage these digital allies wisely and embark on your journey towards achieving peak productivity.

www.ingramcontent.com/pod-product-compliance
Lightning Source LLC
Chambersburg PA
CBHW070943220526
45469CB00007B/2494